Departure 19

For Rod

To my knight in shining logic,
You are the one I come home to.
The one who is my home.
Let's go dancing in the parking lot under the stars,
Kiss me in the rain.
Thank You for taking me to the moon
and the ocean.
My heart glows when you are here.
I love our little adventures.
You're my forever.

For Paul

Thanks for the motorcycle rides
And East coast vibes

For Genevieve

She smiles when you say she's insane.
It's no secret she is mad.
Her soul has a story
that would be one for the ages.

For Mom

I see dragonflies everywhere I go. I know you are always with me. I miss you. I love you.

For Sarah

Boondock Saints and South Boston will always have a place in my heart.

For James

I love you, ocean baby.

For Ashley

We have found *Paradise.*

For Peter

Do you remember me?
I remember you
with your eyes sewed shut
Closed to a world
with no patience for people like us
We found this shelter

There are worlds to battle between
here and there
A destination across the ocean
In the world
Are we the chaos?
Or are we the simplicity?

I have many faces
Even as strangers you saw me
friend
I see you too.

*It's summer
The warm sun glows on my skin
as I lay on my back
in my blue bikini
Palm tree print on each breast
Eyes closed
I feel my skin tingle
each ray of light
lovingly invades my body
Illuminates my spirit
That was in slumber
all winter
I sip on my iced tea
Sleep here on my towel
for another moment
and I don't give a thought
to skin cancer
or sunburn
Because
The feeling
Of
Summer
Is
Addicting*

Salty Fresh
I smell the beach from miles away
I wiggle my toes in the sand
each one is buried
Making castles with my hands
The ocean is blue, baby
I dive in
Give my everything
I let the tide take it away
The white foam on the shore
chases me
and draws me to play
The wind blows my hair
Into a
lovely mess
My rolled-up jeans
are soaked
around the bottom
Collecting seashells along the shore
Sacred treasures
I keep
Ocean, you are my love
Crystal
Blue
Heaven
Sea, everything you do is
Gorgeous
and
Romantic
Nothing's wrong
from now on
This is what I was born to be
Mysterious
Captivating
I am
an
Ocean baby

I'm sobered this summer
My soul is filled with
warm butterflies
When winter comes
I'll be walking on glass
Help me tie my boots
tight tight
I don't want this to end
The lemon sun
and cotton sky
makes me smile
I took the bus alone
and told the couch to stay home
My burning bare feet is all the cement
ever knows
Today is my day
I love my new home

The sun shines on her shoulder
Luminous eyes
She smiles
The moon is wild
Her hips are criminals
I am charged
with a life sentence
Served in a glistening
Silky
inhibition murdering
web
The life I live
The love
The hate
falling into the sea
The fusion of addiction
and euphoria
calculate the hours
until my death
Twinkling
Shimmering
Blinding
Light

I tried to sleep in a new house last night. It was intriguing yet unfamiliar. The windows by my bed were open, letting in a cold draft that was strangely comforting. I folded my pillow in half giving myself a little leverage above the half-aired up blow-up bed. I was able to shut my eyes only to dream about going home. I had way too much on my mind to possibly sleep. In between blinks, film clips played in my mind of the past 2 years and just the past week. It's so exciting to leave everything behind—like the first time trying a drug; I'm not sure how my body will react to these new feelings, but I can't wait to get high on life. I want to walk upstairs, but I'm scared to move further from the door in case I decide to start running in the other direction. The thing about running that can be so satisfying for the moment is it always has the illusion that you are starting over. No furniture, no music blaring, no cartoons playing on the TV, and it's quiet here. It's nothing like your room. This is exactly the kind of noise that I am going to fill the room with anyway wherever it may be on the map. I travel with my heart in a carboard box. I just hope it doesn't rain.

I love her
like the ocean loves the waves
Crashing softly into one another
She is mad
She is frail
She possesses me
Pushes me right to the edge
I welcome the chaos
The girl is weary
Yet captured by the art of it all
She speaks like Shakespeare
Smiles with her eyes
There's an orb of light that follows her
in the dark nights
Peace escapes the mind of a lover
dreaming and wandering
around in a place I cannot go
It's unsafe to love her
but still, I do

Be still
Here
in this moment
I came just to see you
as you are
Take me to your sky
Take me to your depths
I will leave my stain on your soul
Be placid
Here
with me
It's only
Us

The brisk nocturnal air
whispers promises to the stars
To bask in their vast beauty
I wonder where the universe begins
I wonder when forever comes
Will my eyes ever see?
Is there proof
of the truth
My soul stirs
It's a distant kindle
It's a slow
living breathing thing
I cannot seize it
A wonderous
magnificent world

I can feel my soul squirming inside me
Trying to impregnate my body with all that it knows
I seem to be more aware when the world's chaos
sleeps safely inside their homes
When the lights are dim, and I am alone
My words are unattached from my lips
Can you still hear me?
I am not striving for things that society eats
to feed their comfort and thrills
I want something more; I'll keep searching until I find it
Roaming the streets like a vagabond
Collecting aluminum cans
and the pieces I need to fill in the blanks of my story
I will find my place
Home is everywhere
Home is nowhere
Home is a bathroom wall
written on by the ones who have roamed here before
I may travel alone because you are a skeptic
But that's okay. Today is mine, Tomorrow is ours

I'm dragging along my baggage
The question is
Would you like it in paper or plastic?
I am going to take you on the best trip of your life
I need to go for a walk outside
clear my cluttered mind
I can't wrap myself around the reality
of all that I'm leaving behind

Drunk off coffee I sit here inspired
All I want to do is write about nothing
the thoughts inside
sometimes meaningless
But they are mine
The solace moments that make me feel alive
The words cover me like blankets
made from the cotton of my own heaven
I am gullible to the world's intentions
and I try to capture the many colors of a flower
as it makes a kaleidoscope behind my eyes
The sun peeks through the grey sky
a paralyzing beauty
My little paper heart crumbles in the rain
Skin is salty when wet
Memories taste strangely sweet when regurgitated
Still nothing is quite the same
I feel amplified a thousand times when I expose my secrets
I walked to the top of the hill
leaving behind crumbled pieces of cement
The chair underneath the tree beckons me
this is the perfect place to scratch some pages
The sun is shining now
slowly burning a hole into the night
The wind softly brushes my hair to the back of my shoulders
a humble goodbye
A warning that winter is coming
The trees rustle letting me know I have outstayed my welcome
I've been sitting here for hours
barefoot and anemic
My body needs minerals
Orange to red, red to brown
Fall
Fall
Don't leave me summer
I am in love with you

Little color prisms of light that shine through misty water
Wishing flowers
Baby kisses
Warm sheets fresh out of the dryer
These glimpses
These moments
that give you a peek into heaven
This is what it feels like
to find the light
We don't have time
yet it's endless
Coffee at midnight
Thunderstorms
Sunsets
Breathe in
Breathe out
We are mortal
Made of flesh and bones
Feel your heartbeat
Dancing alone in your room because you're in love
Laughing
Fingers streaming through the wind outside the window
on a moonlit drive
Harbor each moment
keep them in your pocket
savor them slowly
Live as if you have hope of seeing more
Live as If you won't

Hands grip the steel
Stomach drops
Heart beats faster
Weightless in the sky
I let go
Forget it all
My eyes blink slow as I stare at the clouds
Let me go
I'll let go
You can't hold me
I am gone
I am free
Don't cage me
Let me go
I'll let go

I caress
the indent of your body on the mattress
I lay awake
listening for the slamming of the front door
I left the key under the mat
Just in case you came home
in case you needed warmth
You have changed
Even your eyes are a different shade of blue
They reflect the sadness in me
I never meant to bring you here
All I wanted to do was keep you
as a piece of art on my wall
I admire you
I cherish you
Let no other woman glance upon the
masterpiece of you
No one knows who we are
inside these four walls
I'll never tell a soul
the secrets you lock away
I miss you
The scent of your hair
The strumming of your guitar
and the sweetness
the bitter taste
of your lips
Come home
and be
a part
of my
antic world

I am like a leaf on her tree
Merely waiting to change colors
and wait for a gust of wind
to make me fall
So that little girls can pick me up and glue me to their diaries

As I am sipping my latte on a cushy couch in the corner café

I notice her

She walks like a panther
with stealth and ambition
Even the way she turns a doorknob
seems to hold a great importance

She's one of those people that walks
instead of runs
in all the right angels
She always seems to be the first one to reach her destination

I am the one who kicks a piece of trash on the street all the
way home
I am proud of this strange victory

This girl reminds me of the one on the cover of a glossy style
magazine
I am equally disgusted as I am curious

I am five and my hands are weak
I can smile more easily

I wish I was twenty

I walk around in shoes too big for me
I wear lip gloss to look pretty
This face will fit me when I'm twenty

I haven't lost my purity
I will when I'm twenty

My feet hurt from working all day
To pay the rent

I haven't slept for a week
My lip-gloss is shiny
Pink
Pretty

Oh, they all want to love me
They all want to break me

when I'm twenty

I wish I could run
somewhere
and never look back

Aren't I glad to be twenty?

You're a compassionate
stranger
that lends me a smile when I am
a vagabond of
bad choices
and
reckless
freedoms
I love losing hope
and getting it back again
with you

Who will play the role of me if my life was a movie?
Would you be the director?
Would it be sad?
Or thrilling?
Don't make me filthy rich or ridiculously hot
I don't want that kind of responsibility

Will the music be chaotic? moving?

The opening scene is a girl on a subway with headphones on
Strange and out of place she makes you wonder...... Where
she's going and what she is thinking in that head of hers.

Make it a super cool indie film

Whatever shirt I mismatch with my socks
Whatever road I travel
Whoever I am
When it's a hand I'm looking for
When you are unaware
that I am even here

I'm still my own

When it rains
When it pours
These are my feet
These are my plans

Not yours

Whatever stupid thing leaks from my lips
Whatever song I play
It's not for you

Whichever side I'm on today
Whosever heart I break

I'm still my own

On the Ferris wheel of dreams
I'm flying high
Ignoring what's below
I'm in another world
I won't come down
My lips are trembling
with words I want to say
My heartbeat skipping away from me
My pulse dancing
My head is dizzy
I'm falling up
I believe in you
We could be perfect
for each other

A blank canvas
A wintry decolorized paradise
Tiny snowflakes trickle down on my nose
I breathe in
My body frigid and still
a silence fills the air
Snow is
Alluring
Inspiring
Renewing
Clean
As I resist the urge to love it
I find myself
in an unexpected
state of felicity

Life is kind of like a complicated game of
chess
I've never learned to play
I'm just staring at the pieces
Pretending to contemplate my next move
The truth is I have no strategies
Only a prayer
Hope
Life is in the moments given a little at a time
I snap a picture
I write its serenade
Reasons
Seasons
and the love that brings you through it all

The world can break you
and I don't know why we feel too much
You must clench your fists
and grasp on to yourself
Humans are humans
They will let you down
You must be careful too
The condition of the heart
is a delicate thing
It's a hard line
to draw between
Flight
And
Fight
Most people see
the meek-hearted
as the weak ones
When they are really
the pulse of it all
Making the world turn
and we understand more
about why we are here
My dear
we don't just exist
we need to feel everything
The weight of the deep water
is heavy
Don't stop swimming
Just
Don't let it take you under

Trade my shoes for ones that fit me
Pick my smile up off the ground
Pour my heart into finding the pieces
that have all been tossed around

I'm just going to be together with myself
cause I am the girl when no one is around

I won't be a fool from what you're showing me
I'm not your property
even if it leaves me in poverty

I am just going to be together with myself

My life
My choice
My heart

If I get lonely
I'll be best friends with the girl I'm going to be
when you're gone

When I paint on my naked canvas
I try to capture

The old man on the bicycle
Little girl
Red balloon
Yellow kite
Saxophone-playing bum

Gazing lost beauty
in contrast to the spinning colors behind her
Clouds shaped like deformed lizards
Smoke filled cafes
Window shoppers
Spilled milk
Gum on the cement
Eyes
Wheels
What a scene this would be
shame I am not a painter
The canvas is my mind
Moving pictures
and it's never about an individual vision
It's a collection of beautiful things
that make the world spin
I never overlook the real Kodak here
The night in New York
The streets I walked
The leaves that fell on my shoes
The rocks I tripped over
The dollar I gave the bum
The smile of the little girl
The gum that stopped me in my tracks to see it all
The wheels of the bus taking me on my next adventure

Time is not a clock on my wall
It's a moment
A collection of moments
that mix together
Their vivid dreams born
Creating a presence
that makes me realize
there is so much more
to this life

You say the stars are beautiful
but you'll never feel beauty until you break one in your hands

The sun dances naked
The clouds keep you wondering
how far the sky expands
meanwhile protecting you from blindness

You can't look beauty head on you see
and happiness is rationed

Rain pours on the heads of people
who refuse to cry
The sweet saturation is vital

The moon plays peek-a-boo
with your glow in the dark heart

I poked holes in the sheets
so, we can do this all night

Love me carefully
as not to tear the fabric of my heart's inevitable disaster
My vibrance has dulled down to a dim light
I'm wearing my rose-colored glasses
Your smile illuminates the darkness
I forget what I was afraid of
You are armored with a sensibility
that chases the grey from my view
The world is a chaos
But here
in this room
all I see is you

My heart beats rhythmically with the pulse of the city
I am unable to focus
I had my arms stretched out beside me
spinning making myself dizzy
I press my lips together tightly
and listen to
The shuffle of footsteps steadily pounding the concrete
The beeping pedestrian lights
Distant birds chirping
Voices bouncing off the steel buildings
I can feel the buzzing
in my bones
Of the electricity
fueling it all

It's the faces
It's the places
that we go
It's faith in all the people that we know
It's the trees
It's the bottom of the sea
It's my memories
slowly fading
It's my life
and it's always changing

The busy streets of New York are bustling in a fast-forward
motion
Taxi cabs honking
Suits wired to cell phones talking to money on the line
A homeless man on the corner
moving at a much slower pace than the rest
My favorite is Tony blowing away on his saxophone
making a soundtrack to this fascinating stage
filled with many diverse characters
Everyone is in a hurry to live
before they die

Here I am
watching it all in amazement and curiosity
My eyes flickering
Glitter filled
I am still
Soaking it all deep into my pores

Observing
I love to stare at others
to feel them
study the way they move
their smell
the lines in which they walk
expressions on faces
The lies they tell
The awful truths
I am a spectator
and when I pass a window
I notice my reflection
A random object
placed in an abstract photograph
It looks like me
only more colorful

Shiny and pretty
you stare at me through the glass of your one-gallon bowl
that sits on top of my lopsided bookshelf
surrounded by cleaning supplies and homework
I am envious of your simple life
but I am guilty of trapping you
Oh well
What do you care?
This is all you've ever known
I gaze out from my third story window
I see the sky half blacked out
by the man fixing the streetlight
and I wonder.......
Am I the one in the glass bowl?

Do you want to be free
like the shadow of a bird
passing a cloud
on its way
to something
he knows not what
but hopes it's something good
Like a ripe apple
The smell is a succulent strawberry
Youthful
Maybe you can run
and not get any further from where you started from
Let's hide
right here
Of course you'll be safe
getting older is on my list of things to do today
Keep in flight
and fly straight in my direction
When you land
ignore the noise
behind
you

I used to think that life was made up of faithful chemicals mixing creating emotion. An emotion that drives us to dream and make plans. I have come to realize that the lines on the map are not as definite as they seem. There are many roads you can take to get to the same place. The why is not as important as the is. The simplest things in life have proven to be the most real. There's no science to love it just happens. There is truth in all the things we don't understand. Intelligence is knowing that you know not.
It's simple.

Unexpected dreams
sneak into
adventurous
hearts

When I walk through the door
I want to be part of the room
Better yet a shiny thing
Then I see you
Maybe I don't really want
to be this chandelier
crashing to the floor

Running naked in the streetlights
swimming chasing moonlight
streams
These are the good times

Midnight
Gazing
Howling wolves cry
It's like flying
Like trying to see through
light
blinding while driving

Breathing
cold air

Hope for me
hope falling
Watching
Waiting
to catch the blessings
Lately they stick
like leaves on a rake
I wish I swam in the pile
I need to feel only the love
Believe me it's real
Stop crushing it
under your heels
I know it's raining glitter
It sparkles
Then lighting strikes
It's all one planet
Thriving like the pulse inside of you

The spectacle of the sunset
paints the illusion of day
Marking the death of hours
Lies and dreams marry each other
Thoughts rest inside
of an effortless slumber
My daily frets
slip under my covers
and love is all that waits
in the dark corners of my room
Memories of the past
and faith in the future
hibernate
inside my breath
When minutes combust and time is limited
I will not be spun
into the world's confusion
All the things that make me feel alive
will be my lullaby

Do you ever wonder who you would be if you just
learned to grow into yourself
I'm afraid of the word statistics
It makes me feel like I'm a number on a barcode
and I'm destined to repeat my history
I can't help but wonder
Will I be someone who watches the news
wears red lipstick
and always smells like cigarettes and cheap perfume
or the kind of person who collects
cats and self-help books
Will I daydream myself
into a world
of irresponsibility
I will feel myself
sinking into my stomach
wishing I could find a way to believe
my own inspirational mantras
"Beauty is on the inside"
but sooner or later I will be buying
push up bras
and gooping gobs of anti-wrinkle cream
and counting calories
or maybe I will look back at these confused
20 something ramblings
and laugh
Laugh at myself

Let me be real
Honest
Brutal
Violently aware
Maybe it won't hurt
to suck the dust
from the windows
in my house
A house built
single handedly
Breakable by a baby's whisper
Let me be a word
that sings like an angel
Wrapped in warm sheets
smelling of summer blooms
straight from a mother's hands

I think the sky is falling
with rain on earth
just like the things between us
You make me angry
You make me shutter
You make me wonder
You make me weaker

and you make it better

I'll stay for hours
I'd better go
There are things you won't tell me
are they better left unsaid?

You make me bitter
You make me honest
You give me shelter

and you make it better

You stay beside me
Leave me alone

You make me feel wanted
You make me feel haunted
I think I hate you
but the problem is
that I don't

I touched my lips but were they mine?
I looked around and wondered....
Is this real?
I washed my face hoping to wash away
some of the dirt that tainted me
But in doing so it only made clearer what was underneath
I looked in the mirror
and stopped like a train had just ran my heart over
with no intent of breaking
I didn't recognize this stranger staring back at me
She looked so lost and so broken
As if she had reached a f nal breaking point in the war against
body and mind
The look on her face was like she had just heard of a death
Her death
The person she knew she was
amongst the disarray
Running her fingers across her bones
searching for sign that she's alive
This must be the lowest feeling
to come to this realization and not having anyone to blame
but yourself
I could almost hear the shattering of hearts
including her own
All the things that were meaningful
seemed to have lost their color
that was the point I knew I lost myself
and I had to find her

I need you to know that I am crazy
I might stare at the sun head on
I might do things you don't understand
I might enclose into myself
I might seem sad
when I am just thinking
Give me some time to sort things out
I don't see the world the same
Abstract
Random
Strange
Gorgeous
I am
alone
Don't be alarmed
this is my normal

She takes pictures
of things
moving past her
moving with her
and she frames them in her dreams
She is all the world has made of her
but inside she is wanting
that something
that innocence
that relevance
Relevant to her
She walks past buildings full of people
still
she's empty
wanting so much more
than still life objects
in her sight
She rolls down the window to revive her broken spirit
stolen by a world that always seems to break her
innocence
Her relevance
that's everything to her

I am a walking disaster
Stumbling
I drop the wine glass
as you stare
with piercing
Exquisite
eyes
College boy sweater
you half smiled at me
And said
Girl, you are a mess
That's me
We babble drunk
talking deep and slow
I ask him
Aren't the fall colors phenomenal?
Yes, they are
Whatever happened to doing this before technology

I suppose I should have known
It gets boring
The very thing
that makes a person so intense
It can exhaust you
The extraordinary
The drama
The shock
The adventure
The intellectual conversation
I'm tired
I feel like watching a stupid cartoon
Just to ease
the fuzziness from my intellectual headache

Put down that dream
interpretation book girl
dreams don't mean a
thing. It's just your mind
making love with itself
spitting out images
you may or may not have
seen in a past life.

We are just passing through here. Our purpose is not to find
sanctity in our bodies. We are supposed to spend a life on a
constant journey to leave a print of our souls here on earth. I
search for love, purpose, peace, significance, and meaning. We
were made for this. Can we will it so? We have hands to touch
and words that have enormous power to build or destroy. Yet
we are weak and become weary. We were all children once.
We knew things then that we forget over time. The innocence
of a child and the heart of her, is the very thing the universe
thrives on. We are all teachers and we are all students. We are
all artists of our own destiny. Some of us are mortal angels on
earth, determined to change the world. We follow a higher
being to guide us along our path. We are all wired with the
human condition. Can we travel these roads together? We
have a much better life to live after these ones. Someday will
be forever.

The night air whispers
secrets of sweet mystery
The pale moon hangs above
waiting
for the sun to sleep
My curiosity lives
inside
My soul
that burns
like the gases of the stars
exploding towards heaven
Lighting the night sky
with the same passionate essence
and beauty
that exists
only in places
beyond humanity
A magic
I see
so deep and pure
On nights like these
I am transformed
as I gaze
at the moon

Tracing moonlit shadows
Searching for the light
Finding

I count the stars
and my blessings

love falling
like rain
on my head

Renewing me

Fireflies fly past
I wait
I watch
I catch them

I let it all
GO

I can't explain why I'm writing and scribbling at 2am or why
faces turn into sketches on my wall.

It's beautiful to collect inspiration in small pieces and write a
story. The pages are in no order.

I dream in color
I write music in my dreams

I rarely remember the melody right away

Like my mind is teasing me

Leaving me with a frustration of creativity
and a ridiculous amount of blank and crumbled up pages.

I feel like a ghost
Like I've been here
longer than twenty years
My body tingles
as I am lifted
into
the purple sky
Tiny organisms
race through my body
as it fights to heal the scars of my past
I feel old.
I am young.

I used to write beautiful LIES
I've lost my voice in an overcrowded art gallery
I just can't express myself the way I want

I don't want to leave unfinished writing around the house for
you to read and misunderstand

I don't want to speak because the words
aren't found
I don't want to fumble

Mess
Things
Up

So, what's your story? You must have one, because you are sitting across the table from me at 3:00am. My story is that I'm just a girl, taking a long drag after a long day, nervously flicking the ashes, many unnecessary times into the ashtray. I am going to slip into the hot shower. It helps me sleep better.
Knock....
Knock...
Why are the lights off in the bathroom?
Because I take showers in the dark
Its relaxing
I pretend I am in an exotic
waterfall
Instead of a house full of college students
You should try it sometime
Close your eyes
and let the water trickle down your spine
I am starring in a sexy music video
Whatever I must do
A daydream
to wash off the pressures of the day.

Don't forget to take your little white pill every morning
Even before you start the coffee pot and smoke your cigarette
because today might just be the day...... you lose your way
Take these pills to detox the intoxication of my mind's tripping
high
I take the pink pill to fight the time war between childhood and
motherhood
Hey Doctor! I don't feel so good
It must be the side effects
of the medication of my frustration living in
this Prozac generation
Hey Doctor!
I don't feel so good
He looked at me and said
"You're so young and have so much light behind your eyes
I know it's confusing, and how do you feel about that?"
I closed my eyes, shook my head, and started laughing
Then he started writing something down on a piece of white
paper.
Hey Doctor!
I don't feel so good
See all my friends have something to hang on the wall that
says who they are. As for me.... I have a map. No, I don't know
where I am going. I only know that I don't want to be here.

This pill
These pills
I'm not so sure anymore what they are all really for

Escaping is much like sleeping in that extra hour just to finish that dream where you were the queen of your own castle. In Some foreign country, where no one knows your afflictions or your addictions. You are redeemed like you've been given a chance to re-create the reputation of your name.... Of your face...

Some people live for the moment, and some of them are just as messed up as I am. There's a kind of strange and comforting feeling that comes from indulging in the fantasy of what could be... We eventually do wake up from this illusion of reality. We realize that what we were experiencing in our dream was a vivid demonstration of regret. An exchange of chaos in the mind and soul. An attempt to re write history and elude the present. My brain chemicals were firing against each other causing my soul to run wild with ideas. The real question I have is: Why doesn't the disappointment of reality hinder our desire to dream? I have wondered this at times when reality has once again slipped away, and I was addicted to the freedom of running away.

I love the feeling of swimming underwater, the liberty of being submerged in something so deep and refreshing. I would live in this deep ocean of myself if it wasn't for the fact that I had to come up for air. I must accept that I cannot breathe here for long in this comforting escape. Life is an incarceration, but there is beauty and soul to be found on land. My feet need to be on dirt to see it here. I cannot let myself drown simply because the feeling of emersion and escape is addicting and soothing. I can go under, but I can't stay long. BLUE WATER escape.

After searching the dark corners of my mind.... I've realized I cannot keep doing this. My choices have consequences. I can't run away forever, not by closing my eyes to the truth and dreaming a different ending. I can't just swallow a pill that has me sleeping on clouds for days. I can't drink until everything is funny. Eventually.... The music stops, I must go home. I must see the bags under my eyes and feel the pain in my body. The next morning after the party, they are all passed out on the lawn like fools getting sunburns when they could have been dancing in the sun. Drugs fade, yet beauty never dies. I won't glorify them anymore. The more I run from reality, the farther behind I get. What I thought was freedom, was the very thing that imprisoned me.

Let's Go
I say
Climb the tallest tower
sit here for hours
Watching people down there
Is it the past that keeps me down?

The pain of growing up
is what I fear

Big city lights
Trees grown wild
Ocean tides
Mountains high

Covered by sky
Sky
Sky

I've met you on the road
on a plane
sat next to you on the train

Then I'm gone again

I would tell you my name
if only I could keep you near

If I do, I'd have to lie
say I'm traveling alone
Truth be told
I'm holding on to all I've ever known

Lucky for you it won't be too long until you see me
again
Look up
up
To the sky
Sky
I'm looking up

At the same
Sky
Sky

There's a lot of things you don't know about me
A part of me always feels like leaving in the middle of the night

Get me on a bus
Get me on the next train
Yeah.... Get me on the next flight

I've got to GO
Yes, right now
60 seconds
say Goodbye

Look for me
I'll be flying
in the
Sky
Sky

Here is my heart
now have a good night

I have stage fright
I don't know when I'm leaving
again
Just that I might
I'm a flight risk
a black sheep
With my head
towards the
Sky
Sky

Get me on a bus
Get me on the next train
Yeah.... Get me on the next flight

It's the fear
of failing
that keeps me running
Chucks on the asphalt

Wheels turning
Stomach churning
My hearts burning

Don't chase after me

Don't worry
I never leave any of you behind
I never do

I'm still here
Are you?

Look up loves
We're looking up at the
same
Sky
Sky

Don't envy me
for what I am
I am looking at you
with admiration too

Where is that girl?
The boy?
You know him?

Picture in my pocket
I keep having the same re occurring dreams
of us

Hotel desires
Frequent fliers
with

perpetual liars

I cover my eyes
to the world
I've been looking all around town for you

They will ask why the shades
are down in the daylight

Tell them to mind their own business

Life is a swinging door
It's like walking barefoot on a squeaking floor
I have my heart in my hands
I'm in over my head
Trying hard to tie the loose ends
Holding my breath
Enclosing the warmth within
Pain is shards of glass
Like photos taken in the dark
blurry and unsharp
Time feels so long
in times of
trouble

What will they think when they find me here? In the corner
watching the room spin alone. Twitching with too much
contemplation.... Book flipped to page one my half-drunk
coffee in my hand. A mellow dramatic song plays on repeat. I
feel small, smaller, and shrinking into the coils of my bed. My
face is colorless. I'm losing heart every day that I allow myself to
regress to child likeness. As a result of my fear of changing. A
fear that these in between stages will leave me alone and
yearning for a more fulfilling life. It feels pathetic. The world
doesn't stop whether I spin with it or not. Stop the cars, people,
and clocks. Stop this ride I want to get off. I want to stand still
and surrounded while I look for a direction to run. I'm trying to
catch up with all that leaves me feeling behind. Stop the whole
world I'm feeling nauseas. I must be the only one... I don't
know. No one else should be reading these late-night
rubbishes. There have been brief, yet relevant moments that I
have felt what it must be like to drown. The furniture was
underwater, the celling was the sky, and with my arms
outstretched I reached for something pure and golden.
I feel like a ghost haunting this house. A supernatural presence
of the person that used to shine with a luminescent smile.

Death and re-birth
Pretending I'm happy
I walk around like a zombie with a smile
My heart is riding passenger in the worlds bumper car
crashing until
I am numb
Nothing hurts anymore
In their eyes
I am vibrant
Young
and have boundless opportunities
I know I will only find it
If I look for it
If I believe in what I know
As long as I am alive
If I choose to ride

Its 3:00 am
Happy hour. I walk into my empty room filled with pictures of my friends in California. I wonder what they are doing. Probably sleeping. I just got home. I stumble trying not to burn my back with my cigarette as I sweetly slip out of my little fringy black dress. Half empty iced coffee in one hand I flick my long ash into a watery chicken substance leftover from the noodles I reluctantly ate for the thousandth time yesterday. I need to find a way to embrace the half-light in my room. I'm buzzing from the night before. I'll do it all over again today. I'll work two jobs, go to school, and go dancing all night.

My heart was a piece of ice
not cold
Just frozen
Here
inside this place
I created for you
The heat between our bodies
could have melted it
It wasn't the right time
My only hope is that you'll
remember me
For what I felt for you
Like an old friend
that you had forgotten their name
until they smiled
Until I smile again
Goodbye

It smells like cleaner and plastic here
I sit in my charcoal stained jeans
Why does everything have to be a freaking poem?
It's a twisted form of inspiration
It's just not healthy to wake from sleep
To compose music or write about the psych hospital

Paper pants
Paper pants

Ativan
Ativan

Hard restraints
Soft restraints

Paper pants
Paper pants

Ativan
Ativan

Hard restraints
Soft restraints

This song is stupid

I lit a candle in my room while listening to Frou Frou
A flicker of light lit up a picture of us
Like a shrine of regret
It's hard to look at myself this way
see photos of a better time
A time when I didn't know what it felt like to be used
I feel like a small animal
One you want to cuddle with
yet also prey upon

Up until now I thought insanity was something I had to worry
about when I was old. Talking to my grandchildren in a senile
tone. I was wrong... Insanity can come at any age. The feeling
that you are out of control. It's unmanageable and self-rotating
in a circle of repetition.
Self-destructing now......
5...4....3...2...1!

Your name is still written on the wall
from when you were here
What is keeping me?
Why do I keep coming back?
Is it my love for you?
It is sick
You are the only one there to pick me up
after you knock me down
So far
all I see is up
No sideways or slouching
in my view
You have no idea what this looks like
I know you've been here
See
Here is your name
written all over my face
For some reason that makes me feel like a celebrity
somehow
Cleaner
more beautiful
Because I belong to someone

It seems I am immune
Things aren't always as they seem
I am not immune
I am numb
Novocain
My foot is asleep

It doesn't matter
It should matter
It used to matter

It made me angry
I used to fight
I used to fly

But now...
It's gone

If this is love
Then love is death
You have been killing it
sucking up
my air
with every breath
of sweet nothings

Here I am again with my head in my hands, feeling faceless in the company of my friends. My soul loved by the world. I wish I could see what they see...to save myself from me. Some people have tried to make me magically fearless with their plans. You know just as well as I do, there is no fun in that. I've always wanted to travel but I guess I thought there would always be someone to help me carry my bags. My eyes are faded as I stare, chasing a distant light. I am trying so hard to convince myself that yes, in fact these shadows are mine. It's like flipping through channels late at night and finding yourself watching infomercials of useless things you'll never buy. These are the delete worthy stories of my life. I act, tell, and portray but the lens is out of focus. I would make a point if I could just remember what it was, I wanted to say. There are swirls of color mixing in my brain. An array of things I haven't the strength to explain, so I will just pour them out like Picasso.

I feel like the bath water we draw up together will always be awkward and lukewarm.

Love will always be bittersweet.

I want to become content without becoming a still life piece of art. My contentment only exists somewhere in the middle. Will someone please meet me in the middle just to remind me that my journey is not so aimless. I just need a friend to walk the distance with me.

Reading Vogue
Gold-trimmed shoes
Funky blue eyeshadow
She sits across from me on the bus
I can't help but notice her lips pursed together
Making her look glamorously uncomfortable

Yellow socks
Black boots
Leggings with scribbles in sharpie
Shredded skirt
Red striped football tee
Original
Fashionable
Artist
Heart
Passion
Poetry
I
Love
Her

I wonder if Emily
Dickinson
or William Shakespeare
had scraps of paper all
over the house

Hot tea
Coffee
Conversations
Painting
Truth
Heart evoking
Glowing faces
Breathing
Nature
Sleeping
Bonfires
Tin cans
Tin can man
Collecting seashells
Moments
Sunsets
Passion

The sky makes me feel alive
I am happy
The moments pass quickly
I am a traveler

Time only exists merely for salvation. I hope one day I will find myself inside this skin and maybe one sunset, I will have the patience to wait for the moon's arrival. When I am in this position, I'll know what to do. I'll stay in one place long enough to marvel at the stars and contemplate their relevance to me and my unfortunate gravity.

The grass isn't
greener on
the other side
It's just wetter
and stains
your jeans

I put my hand out to feel the warm breeze out of the car window as I watch the flickers of light shine through the tall redwood trees. The mountain air smells fresh and clean. I peek down the winding road and realize how high I have traveled. The music in my ears plays a soundtrack to this beautiful mystery. White snow falls. I sit still and listen to the owls and the pitter patter of deer rustling in the forest.

Underwater Blue
Sand falling slowly through my fingers
Lemon sun and orange sky
Fireflies glow green
Floating pieces of dandelions
Wish
Rain
Grey
Starfish squish
Whales hum
Dolphins click
Snow melt
Refresh
Fog
Dim light
Tunnels
Bridges
Babbling brook
Raging waterfall
Falling rose petals
Flock of birds
Umbrellas on a windy day
Waves crashing against rocks
Ocean cove
Belly dancers
Magenta
Gold
Stars
Coffee shops
Indie Films

The sun is fading
A kiss goodbye to summer
My hips sway back and forth
like wind through the trees
My eyes are filled with stars
I smile at you
Draw you in
with my majestic blue eyes
If there was ever a time you wanted me
Now is the time to be with me

TWENTIES LIFE CRISIS

Your body is a temple
Am I too unholy?
I desire you

If love is suicide to reason
Then I would die
Dive into your skin
Past your bones
Right to your soul

Cause you are the only one
that opens the door
to my heart
You are the only one
who sings my songs

Beauty
Body
Envy the girl
catches your thrill
Just like all the other girls
who don't love you
Letters poems pictures
in your past
Am I still a beauty?
Is she new?
You will break her
I am the girl
you wanted
just as much as the other untouchables
I am still touchable
I said yes
Fell in love
Tears fall
You know she isn't different
add her to the list of girls
who confuse you
You want better
Honey
Baby
Lovely
You had it in me
More sex
Beauty
Perfect body
More thrills
More tears
It's not fair
I'm the one who showed them
your handsomeness
But they'll never see it
like I do

Don't look down
Take your time
Breathe with me

Don't worry my friend
I'll save your place in line
until your ready again

It doesn't matter what they think
I'll tell them your sleeping

It gets better
Don't go on pretending

We're not lovers.
We're not friends. We
are just two strangers
with a fantastic secret
life.

She loves to paint
Paint her face
Not because she wants to hide
It doesn't always suit her
She wants you to stare at her
Like a stranger stares at an artist's masterpiece
He passes it, something catches his eye
At first, he's not sure why
So, he stops to admire it
The first thing he sees is its beauty
Then he studies it. He notices a detail that startles him
maybe it's ugly
or abstract like in a Picasso.
His curiosity is driven further
Next, he discusses it with a fellow art lover.
The two of them discuss their interpretations.
They comment on the texture, colors, and meaning.
After the discussion comes the decision
Am I intrigued by this?
One man says it's too chaotic for him
While the other takes it home
To have her love hanging on his apartment wall.

Sleeping in your daydream

A wavelike yearning

Yellow daffodils

In the Morning